INTRODUCT ANATOMY AND PHYSIOLOGY REVISION MADE EASY

A Study tool for an effective learning

By

Anthonia Jones

Table of content

INTRODUCTION

Introduction to anatomy and physiology revision made easy is a book that serves as a revision guide and a study aid to student of various categories, it's a book that has **three sections**,section 1, 2 and 3. **Section 1** contains a brief revision on the introduction to anatomy and physiology , these helps you to recall or revise what you have been taught on the introductory part of anatomy and physiology which also include levels of organization, homeostasis and some important anatomical terms.**Section 2** contains many revision questions and exam questions on the introduction to anatomy and physiology,these make you to access yourself to see if you truly understand the concept of the topic and it also help you to put the topic in your memory,this is based on the theory of exercise which says that we tend to memorize what we practice, so practice makes perfection,the more you practise the more you know more,this book has many examination question that helps you practise and test your understanding on the topic.Section 3 contains the answers to the questions in section 2 this makes you to check if you on the right track by checking if your answer is correct or not.

NOTE: PLEASE FIRST TRY THE QUESTIONS IN SECTION 2 THEN CHECK IF YOU ARE CORRECT TO MAKE THE LEARNING EXPERIENCE AN EFFECTIVE ONE.

SECTION 1

INTRODUCTION TO ANATOMY AND PHYSIOLOGY BRIEF REVISION.

ANATOMY: Anatomy is about studying the parts that make up our bodies and how they work together. There are different areas within anatomy, like Gross anatomy, Microscopic anatomy, Developmental anatomy, and Embryology.

- Gross anatomy looks at body parts without needing a microscope.
- Systemic anatomy studies how organs work together in a system.

- Regional anatomy focuses on specific body regions. Both systemic and regional approaches help us understand gross anatomy.
- Microscopic anatomy, also called *Histology*, uses microscopes to look at the tiny tissues that make up our organs.

PHYSIOLOGY: This field focuses on understanding how different parts of the body work. The connection between structure and function is essential, as how something works depends on how it's built.

HOMEOSTASIS: When the structure and function work together, the body maintains a stable internal environment, known as homeostasis. Even though the external surroundings change, a healthy body's internal conditions stay within normal ranges.

LEVELS OF ORGANIZATION: There are six levels at which the human body can be studied, as it's composed of various parts.

1. Basic Elements:

a. Atoms are the simplest units.

b. Molecules consist of two or more atoms.

c. Inside cells, there are larger molecules called macromolecules.

2. Organelles are groups of macromolecules that have specific roles within cells.

3. Cells are the fundamental building blocks of life with distinct functions.

4. Tissues are clusters of cells working together.

5. Organs: These are made up of different tissues and perform specific functions.

6. Systems: Organs come together to form systems that carry out particular tasks.

7. Organism: All 11 body systems collaborate, creating a functioning organism.

ANATOMICAL TERMS

✧ ANATOMICAL POSITION:

Imagine the starting point for all descriptions of the body. The body stands straight, facing forward, with arms down at the sides, palms forward, and feet together.

✧ DIRECTIONAL TERMS:

We use these special words to talk about where body parts are compared to others.

Medial: When something is closer to the middle of the body. Like how the heart is medial to the humerus (upper arm bone).

Lateral: When something is farther from the middle or on the side of the body. For example, the humerus is lateral to the heart.

Proximal: This means nearer to where a part connects or starts. For instance, the femur (thigh bone) is proximal to the fibula (calf bone).

Distal: This is the opposite of proximal. It means farther away from where a part connects or starts. The fibula is distal to the femur.

Anterior or Ventral: When a part is closer to the front of the body. Like how the sternum (breastbone) is anterior to the vertebrae (backbones).

Posterior or Dorsal: This is the opposite of anterior. It's when a part is closer to the back of the body. The vertebrae are posterior to the sternum.

Superior: Something is higher up or closer to the head. For example, the skull is superior to the scapulae (shoulder blades).

Inferior: This is the opposite of superior. It means something is lower down or farther from the head. The scapulae are inferior to the skull.

✧ BODY PLANES

Three body planes intersect each other at right angles.

These planes partition the body into distinct sections,

enabling the visualization and explanation of its internal

structure from varying viewpoints. The anatomical

position, previously described, serves as the baseline

reference for discussing body planes.

1. Sagittal plane:

Divides the body into left and right halves.

The mid-sagittal plane splits the body into perfectly equal

left and right portions.

The para-sagittal plane divides the body into uneven left

and right sections.

2. Coronal plane:

A coronal or frontal section runs longitudinally,
separating the body into its anterior (front) and posterior
(back) parts.

3. **Transverse plane**:

A transverse or horizontal section produces a cross-
sectional view, separating the body or body segment into
upper and lower components. This section can be taken
at various levels, such as through the cranial cavity,
thorax, abdomen, a limb, or an organ.

✧ **BODY CAVITIES AND THEIR CONTENTS**

Body cavities are spaces within an organism that house
its organs. These cavities are lined with cell layers and
contain fluid, providing protection to the organs while the
organism moves. Commonly referred to as the viscera,

body cavities encompass four main types: cranial, thoracic, abdominal, and pelvic.

1. **Cranial Cavity**: This cavity accommodates the brain and is defined by the following skull bones:

- Anteriorly: Frontal bone
- Laterally: Temporal bones (2)
- Posteriorly: Occipital bone
- Superiorly: Parietal bones (2)
- Inferiorly: Parts of the frontal, temporal, occipital bones, along with the sphenoid and ethmoid bones.

2. **Thoracic Cavity**: Positioned in the upper part of the torso, this cavity is enclosed by the thoracic cage and associated muscles. Boundaries include:

- Anteriorly: Sternum and rib cartilages

- Laterally: Twelve pairs of ribs and intercostal muscles

- Posteriorly: Thoracic vertebrae

- Superiorly: Neck-root structures

- Inferiorly: Dome-shaped diaphragm muscle.

Contents of the thoracic cavity consist of vital structures such as the trachea, bronchi, lungs, heart, aorta, vena cavae, esophagus, lymph vessels, nodes, and key nerves. The mediastinum, the space between the lungs, houses structures like the heart, esophagus, and blood vessels.

3. **Abdominal Cavity**: The largest cavity, oval in shape, occupies a significant portion of the trunk. Its boundaries encompass:

- Superiorly: Diaphragm (separating it from thoracic cavity)

- Anteriorly: Muscles of the anterior abdominal wall

- Posteriorly: Lumbar vertebrae and muscles of the posterior wall

- Laterally: Lower ribs and abdominal wall muscles

- Inferiorly: Continuation into the pelvic cavity.

Conventionally divided into nine regions, the abdominal cavity facilitates the description of organ positions. It contains digestive system components like the stomach, small and large intestines, liver, gall bladder, bile ducts, pancreas, spleen, kidneys, adrenal glands, along with numerous blood vessels, lymph vessels, nerves, and lymph nodes.

4. **Pelvic Cavity**: Resembling a funnel shape, this cavity extends from the lower abdomen and is defined by:

- Superiorly: Continuation from the abdominal cavity

- Anteriorly: Pubic bones

- Posteriorly: Sacrum and coccyx

- Laterally: Innominate bones

- Inferiorly: Pelvic floor muscles.

Within the pelvic cavity, structures encompass the sigmoid colon, rectum, anus, parts of the small intestine, urinary bladder, ureters, urethra, and in females, reproductive organs like the uterus, uterine tubes, ovaries, and vagina. In males, the prostate gland, seminal vesicles, spermatic cords, deferent ducts, ejaculatory ducts, and shared urethra for reproductive and urinary systems are housed.

SECTION 2

REVISIONS QUESTIONS ON INTRODUCTION TO ANATOMY AND PHSIOLOGY

MULTIPLE CHOICE QUESTIONS

1. Gross anatomy involves studying body parts:
a) Under a microscope
b) Without a microscope
c) Only in deceased individuals
d) In isolation from each other

2. Which type of anatomy uses microscopes to examine tissues?
a) Gross anatomy
b) Microscopic anatomy
c) Developmental anatomy
d) Embryology

3. Systemic anatomy focuses on:

a) Individual cells

b) Specific body regions

c) The relationship between structure and function

d) How body parts work together in systems

4. Which of the following is NOT a level of organization in the human body?

a) Organelles

b) Cells

c) Atoms

d) Microorganisms

5. Organs are composed of:

a) Atoms

b) Cells

c) Tissues

d) Organelles

6. What is the primary focus of physiology?

a) Studying body parts and their structure

b) Understanding how body parts work together

c) Analyzing body cavities

d) Examining the microscopic details of cells

7. Homeostasis refers to:

a) The study of anatomy and physiology

b) Maintaining a stable internal environment

c) The process of cell division

d) The body's response to external stimuli

8. The connection between structure and function is essential in physiology because:

a) Structure has no impact on function

b) Function determines structure

c) Structure and function are unrelated

d) They are two separate fields of study

9. How many levels of organization are there in the human body?

a) 4

b) 5

c) 6

d) 7

10. What does the term "organism" refer to in the context of physiology?

a) A collection of tissues

b) A single cell

c) All body systems working together

d) A group of organs

11. Which of the following best describes anatomical position?

a) Lying down with arms at sides

b) Arms raised above the head

c) Standing with feet apart

d) Standing upright with arms at sides and palms forward

12. Medial means:

a) Closer to the head

b) Farther from the midline

c) Closer to the middle of the body

d) Farther from the body's front

13. What is the opposite of proximal?

a) Medial

b) Lateral

c) Superior

d) Distal

14. Which term describes a part that is closer to the back
   of the body?

a) Anterior

b) Medial

c) Lateral

d) Posterior

15. Superior refers to a position that is:

a) Lower down

b) Farther from the head

c) Closer to the feet

d) Higher up

16. Which plane divides the body into left and right
    halves?

a) Coronal

b) Sagittal

c) Transverse

d) Longitudinal

17. A transverse plane divides the body into:

a) Front and back portions

b) Upper and lower portions

c) Left and right portions

d) Anterior and posterior portions

18. What is housed within the cranial cavity?

a) Stomach

b) Brain

c) Lungs

d) Heart

19. Which body cavity contains the kidneys, spleen, and
    digestive organs?

a) Thoracic cavity

b) Abdominal cavity

c) Pelvic cavity

d) Cranial cavity

20. The mediastinum is a space found within the:

a) Abdominal cavity

b) Cranial cavity

c) Thoracic cavity

d) Pelvic cavity

21. What is the primary focus of developmental anatomy?

a) Studying body parts without a microscope

b) Examining tissues under a microscope

c) Understanding how organs work together

d) Investigating the growth and development of
organisms

22. Microscopic anatomy is also known as:

a) Systemic anatomy

b) Gross anatomy

c) Histology

d) Embryology

23. Which anatomical approach helps us understand body
    parts within specific regions?

a) Systemic anatomy

b) Microscopic anatomy

c) Regional anatomy

d) Embryology

24. Which level of organization is composed of groups of
    macromolecules with specific functions?

a) Cells

b) Tissues

c) Organelles

d) Systems

25. What level of organization is formed by organs working together to carry out particular tasks?

a) Cells

b) Organelles

c) Tissues

d) Systems

26. Homeostasis is best described as:

a) The study of body structures

b) Maintaining a dynamic internal environment

c) The process of cell division

d) Adapting to external changes

27. Which term refers to the study of the function of living organisms?

a) Anatomy

b) Physiology

c) Histology

d) Embryology

28. How does homeostasis help the body respond to changes in the external environment?

a) By preventing any internal changes

b) By keeping internal conditions constant

c) By encouraging rapid cell division

d) By increasing metabolism

29. Which level of organization encompasses all the others?

a) Organelles

b) Cells

c) Tissues

d) Organism

30. What is the primary purpose of the respiratory system?

a) Digestion of food

b) Pumping blood throughout the body

c) Regulation of body temperature

d) Exchange of gases between the body and the environment

31. Proximal refers to a position that is:

a) Closer to the head

b) Farther from the midline

c) Nearer to the point of attachment

d) Located posteriorly

32. What is the opposite of lateral?

a) Medial

b) Distal

c) Proximal

d) Superior

33. What anatomical term describes a part that is closer
    to the feet?

a) Inferior

b) Superior

c) Anterior

d) Proximal

34. In the anatomical position, the thumbs are oriented:

a) Away from the body

b) Towards the body

c) Laterally

d) Posteriorly

35. The transverse plane divides the body into:

a) Front and back portions

b) Upper and lower portions

c) Left and right portions

d) Medial and lateral portions

36. Which type of anatomy studies the development of
    embryos?

a) Gross anatomy

b) Microscopic anatomy

c) Developmental anatomy

d) Regional anatomy

37. What is the study of the body's internal structures
    during surgical procedures called?

a) Histology

b) Anatomy

c) Physiology

d) Surgery

38. What does the field of embryology primarily focus on?

a) The study of adult organ functions

b) The growth and development of organisms before birth

c) The study of microscopic tissues

d) The study of tissues in deceased individuals

39. Which level of organization involves the combination of different organs working together?

a) Cells

b) Organelles

c) Systems

d) Tissues

40. Which of the following is NOT an example of a system in the human body?

a) Skeletal system

b) Digestive system

c) Cellular system

d) Respiratory system

41. Which of the following is NOT a function of the
    cardiovascular system?

a) Transporting oxygen and nutrients

b) Pumping blood throughout the body

c) Producing hormones

d) Removing waste products

42. The process of breaking down food into absorbable
    components is primarily carried out by the:

a) Respiratory system

b) Nervous system

c) Digestive system

d) Muscular system

43. What is the primary role of the nervous system?

a) Maintaining homeostasis

b) Pumping blood

c) Providing structural support

d) Transmitting and processing information

44. Which system is responsible for producing offspring?

a) Endocrine system

b) Reproductive system

c) Lymphatic system

d) Muscular system

45. Homeostasis is essential for:

a) Maintaining a constantly changing internal environment

b) Responding to external stimuli only

c) Keeping the body's internal conditions stable

d) Causing rapid cellular growth

46. The term "ventral" is synonymous with:

a) Posterior

b) Anterior

c) Superior

d) Lateral

47. Which directional term describes a part farther away from the surface?

a) Superficial

b) Deep

c) Medial

d) Proximal

48. In which anatomical position are the palms facing backwards?

a) Supine

b) Prone

c) Lateral

d) Anatomical

49. The anatomical term "inferior" refers to a part that is:

a) Above another part

b) Closer to the head

c) Further from the body's midline

d) Below another part

50. The plane that divides the body into equal left and right halves is called the:

a) Transverse plane

b) Coronal plane

c) Sagittal plane

d) Longitudinal plane

THEORY QUESTIONS

1) Explain the difference between gross anatomy and microscopic anatomy. Provide examples for each.

2) Describe the concept of homeostasis and how it is maintained in the human body.

3) What is the relationship between structure and function in the context of anatomy and physiology?

4) Briefly explain the six levels of organization in the human body, from atoms to the organism level.

5) How does the systemic approach to anatomy differ from the regional approach? Give an example of each.

6) Define histology and explain its significance in understanding human anatomy.

7) Discuss the role of the cardiovascular system in maintaining homeostasis within the body.

8) Describe the process of digestion and its importance for providing nutrients to the body.

9) How does the nervous system contribute to communication and coordination in the human body?

10) Explain the significance of the reproductive system in terms of perpetuating the species.

11) Define the anatomical term "superior" and provide an example of a body part described using this term.

12) Discuss the importance of the anatomical position in describing body structures and their relationships.

13) What are directional terms, and how are they used to describe the location of body parts?

14) Describe the functions of the thoracic and abdominal cavities, including the organs they contain.

15) Explain how the three body planes (sagittal, coronal, and transverse) are used to visualize internal structures.

16) What are the key differences between the cranial and pelvic cavities in terms of location and contents?

17) Discuss the role of the endocrine system in regulating various bodily functions through hormone secretion.

18) How does the muscular system contribute to movement and support within the body?

19) Explain the significance of the concept "form follows function" in understanding anatomy and physiology.

20) Describe the importance of understanding anatomical terms and body planes for medical professionals.

SECTION 3

ANSWERS TO THE QUESTION

MULTIPLE CHOICE QUESTIONS ANSWERS

1. b) Without a microscope

2. b) Microscopic anatomy

3. b) Specific body regions

4. d) Microorganisms

5. c) Tissues

6. b) Understanding how body parts work together

7. b) Maintaining a stable internal environment

8. b) Function determines structure

9. c) 6

10. c) All body systems working together

11. d) Standing upright with arms at sides and palms forward

12. c) Closer to the middle of the body

13. d) Distal

14. d) Posterior

15. d) Higher up

16. b) Sagittal

17. b) Upper and lower portions

18. b) Brain

19. b) Abdominal cavity

20. c) Thoracic cavity

21. d) Investigating the growth and development of organisms

22. c) Histology

23. c) Regional anatomy

24. b) Tissues

25. d) Systems

26. b) Maintaining a dynamic internal environment

27. b) Physiology

28. b) By keeping internal conditions constant

29. d) Organism

30. d) Exchange of gases between the body and the environment

31. c) Nearer to the point of attachment

32. a) Medial

33. a) Inferior

34. b) Towards the body

35. b) Upper and lower portions

36. c) Developmental anatomy

37. d) Surgery

38. b) The growth and development of organisms before birth

39. c) Systems

40. c) Cellular system

41. c) Producing hormones

42. c) Digestive system

43. d) Transmitting and processing information

44. b) Reproductive system

45. c) Keeping the body's internal conditions stable

46. b) Anterior

47. b) Deep

48. a) Supine

49. d) Below another part

50. c) Sagittal plane

ANSWERS TO THE THEORY QUESTIONS

1. Gross anatomy involves studying body parts without the need for a microscope, focusing on larger structures visible to the naked eye. Microscopic anatomy (histology) uses microscopes to examine tiny tissues that make up organs.

2. Homeostasis refers to the body's ability to maintain a stable internal environment despite external changes. It involves feedback mechanisms that regulate variables such as temperature, blood sugar, and pH levels.

3. The relationship between structure and function is that the way something is built (its structure) determines how it functions. For example, the structure of the heart's chambers allows it to pump blood efficiently.

4. The six levels of organization in the human body are atoms, molecules, organelles, cells, tissues, organs, and systems, which collectively form the organism.

5. Systemic anatomy studies how organs work together in systems (e.g., cardiovascular system), while regional anatomy focuses on specific body regions (e.g., the head). An example of systemic anatomy is studying the heart's role in circulation, while an example of regional anatomy is studying the various structures in the neck.

6. Histology is the study of microscopic tissues, which helps in understanding the cellular composition and organization of different body parts.

7. The cardiovascular system transports oxygen, nutrients, and hormones throughout the body, maintains blood pressure, and contributes to temperature regulation.

8. Digestion is the process of breaking down food into smaller molecules that can be absorbed and used by the body. It involves mechanical and chemical processes that occur in the digestive tract.

9. The nervous system processes and transmits information through nerve impulses, allowing communication between different parts of the body and coordinating responses to stimuli.

10. The reproductive system is responsible for producing offspring. In males, it involves the production and delivery of sperm; in females, it involves the production of eggs and the nurturing of a developing fetus.

11. "Superior" refers to a body part being higher up or closer to the head. For example, the head is superior to the chest.

12. The anatomical position is a standardized reference point for describing body structures. It involves standing upright, facing forward, arms at the sides, and palms forward.

13. Directional terms are used to describe the location of body parts in relation to other parts. For example, "anterior" means toward the front of the body, and "distal" means farther from the point of attachment.

14. The thoracic cavity contains the heart, lungs, and major blood vessels. The abdominal cavity houses digestive organs, while the pelvic cavity contains reproductive organs and parts of the urinary and digestive systems.

15. Sagittal divides the body into left and right halves, coronal divides it into front and back portions, and transverse divides it into upper and lower parts.

16. The cranial cavity contains the brain, while the pelvic cavity houses reproductive organs, urinary bladder, and part of the large intestine.

17. The endocrine system regulates bodily functions by releasing hormones into the bloodstream. Hormones act as chemical messengers to influence various target cells and organs.

18. The muscular system allows movement, maintains posture, generates heat, and supports other bodily functions.

19. "Form follows function" means that an organism's shape or structure is adapted to its specific role or function in its environment.

20. Understanding anatomical terms and body planes is crucial for clear communication among medical professionals, accurate diagnoses, and effective treatment planning.

Printed in Great Britain
by Amazon

31551521R00030